THE LAST 4 THINGS

AHSAHTA PRESS

The New Series

NUMBER 31

THE LAST 4 THINGS

KATE GREENSTREET

 AHSAHTA PRESS

BOISE STATE UNIVERSITY • BOISE • IDAHO • 2009

Ahsahta Press, Boise State University
Boise, Idaho 83725-1525
http://ahsahtapress.boisestate.edu
http://ahsahtapress.boisestate.edu/books/greenstreet2/greenstreet2.htm

Copyright © 2009 by Kate Greenstreet
Printed in the United States of America
Cover design by M & K Greenstreet
Book design by Janet Holmes
First printing September 2009
ISBN-13: 978-1-934103-09-8

Library of Congress Cataloging-in-Publication Data

Greenstreet, Kate.
  The last 4 things / Kate Greenstreet.
    p. cm. -- (The new series ; no. 31)
  "This book contains a DVD."
  ISBN-13: 978-1-934103-09-8 (pbk. : alk. paper)
  ISBN-10: 1-934103-09-8 (pbk. : alk. paper)
  I. Title. II. Title: Last four things.
  PS3607.R4666L37 2009
  811'.6--DC22

                        2009016978

ACKNOWLEDGMENTS

Thanks to the editors of the journals where parts of *The Last 4 Things* first appeared:
*Absent, Cannibal, Dusie, Fascicle, Filling Station, Konundrum Engine Literary Review,
Kulture Vulture, The Laurel Review, The Literary Review, Spell, string of small machines,
Typo,* and *26 Magazine.*

And thanks to Maggie Schwed for allowing me to use some sentences and phrases from
her side of our correspondence (on pages 19 and 52).

CONTENTS

THE LAST 4 THINGS

The first leaves fell this morning
(my own eyes)

To leave home without making the bed,
it's like building a house of cards.

You have to know what you're doing.
Or be lucky. Or just very quiet.

I have had a Letter from another World . . .

To speak of method. Empathy. Our times, time.
Disappears with me. Sleep a minute.

Empathy is marked with
incomprehensible corrections. The camera must be open.

I know what I tell myself. Sometimes he seems to be the camera
(who we will be later).

Do you like boats? I see you around boats.
Built around an unseen principle: to float.
He's come such a long way to think.

To bring to a stop and keep standing at the edge, when death won't
take you. Hundreds of children.

The camera turns the corner. We're never any closer.
Sometimes he is the camera.

She was trying not
to use beautiful.

"People"
and "life" were problems too.

"Death,"
too. She was vague

about how she would live.
We did some dyeing on my birthday

and took apart some slacks
and skirts from Goodwill, for the wool.

We had the four ages of man, the oceans . . .
There was a likelihood of

hidden problems.
I wanted words, the look,

but everything they meant
seemed wrong.

It had been hard to get the numbers
of deaths. Perhaps you pass under a branch?

Often is a change of direction.

We were on a mountain road.
There is above all this actual place.

Rain was falling and we went off the road.
We were falling but we didn't hit.

This place has a glimpse.
And it seemed that we were held somehow.

Very beautiful showed the lie.

We began with blue. It had seemed
some kind of sky blue.

Dreams a friend, made
of the same stuff as the dark.

No one saw anybody writing something down in all that time.
Later, she could read and she could walk.

We don't know what it means but we do know that the person disappears.

The bridge
attracts us with its brightness.
This map depicts the location.

His little girl sat down on my lap, said: Are you our mommy now?

Consciousness does not affect the body, but exists in a powerless, neutral state. Things that aren't possible come to pass.

You speak of rocks—or a glimpse of blue lake . . .

You have either passed through the shoals or you are entering the shoals. (They ask for predictions.)

Days go by
in the French style,
haiku "postcard" style.

We shall not all sleep, but we shall all be changed.

We were in the fields,
cutting the corn.

We ran through the village,
we thought there was a fire.

That was a hot summer
when the war was over.

Hello
They stop to say hello

Is he crying
He's one of the people

Carrying a pathway
A sacred heart on every wall

It isn't that he can't
pull the trigger

Countries try to hold on
to the little ones

Dust gathers
in the corners, shifting dust

Find a house
Communities of people still exist

If I could choose?
Something modest.

12,000 lbs. of total recall.
Is it a funeral? a dance? politics?

The ghosts look cold. He
carries it hard.

Such a tiny thing, but a black chair would be somber.
Unstable. Disfigured by anger.

In that time frame, little shards appear,
trying to be teeth. A condition formed

by countless mysterious malfunctions.
It becomes the fall you take.

Walk past it all again. Bridge of Fists, Bridge of Straw.
The Bridge of the Honest Woman.

Dear, I will remain here when you go
(I was always saying)

Background? The liquid form
we call water. The blue is in the world.

Something is wrong with the women and the men.
Stone is stronger. "My body is on fire."

That 'existence' was 'pain,' another list of *fors*.
The first divided by the second is equal to the third,
divided by the fourth.

the four corners
suits
the seasons
fire air earth
directions
water
north south west
the gospels
east
your body
lay
like a moat
a weakness for blue

light blown thin
and blurry, like the picture of the glass and the book

There is a chart for America.

flesh
and blood
strong winds

A part of the world can't be visited.

We worshipped these names as the names of our gods—
the woman's high heel, the giant bug, the little viking hat.
I only have my personality to work with.

The people on your train,
some of them get off at your stop.
At least one is upside down.

Each tone, each color, has a different vibration. Everything was getting darker, "dimensional." A woman came here once and fell. To her knees—it was a Sunday, I'll never forget it. In those days, I was very small. I knew my own grief to be so small, nobody could find it. In winter, just the pilings, ropes; ice in black water, "as seen."

All these shots are locked down. I can manage when the pressure is steady—packed with dark-tent, chemical boxes and the camera, an umbrella, a lamp. We talked about colors so much. Or sometimes I feel that the LIFE is there, waiting—but I don't have the part. I know that everything can't be important. They let me take down the curtains. Everything is slightly hidden from me, all the time. It's dark. Did you sleep?

Someone's yelling out there. Have I run out of luck? It's dark—that always takes me back. Rereading our old mail. I have to try, don't I? When you asked me about having a secret, I thought it was just a form of greeting.

Big open double doors, square
of light. Rectangle of light.

"Have you ever had a sleeping dream about the neighborhood?"

In heavy coats, men mass
on the sidewalk.
Ponies who could speak
choose not to. A watch
with water in the face.
Thank you for the pears. Burned
in her presence.

Luckily, our souls don't need protection.
The main thing is, to keep them interested.

Try to keep them near the body.

—What's that? Is he taking pictures?
—No. Lightning. This is real.

Another piece of good advice
I've seen it

over where the couch used to be

          Will exist
    have their beginnings, will please
       (It *means* I will please)

Important hours of the sunlit day
              through willows

I crossed a shallow channel.

Mostly there were hours of deep shoveling.
I encountered rocks
and buried metal.

Standing in the turned-over ground, comes a shadow.
Am I weakening myself?

Early discussions about bridging a river.
Primitive means
of crossing.

She had been there,
the first to leave the village.

Henceforth, the highest thing.
Teleport an object.

Teleport yourself
a short distance (the contemplated work).

Before the bridge was built,
the early bridge,

I never knew where I was.
I was turned, in another direction
so long. I wanted to explain.

Teleport yourself a long distance.
No one imagined
how long you'd sleep.

I wanted to explain—
it didn't mean that I was turning away.

The canals with their black reflections, blacker than asphalt ...

Black ... and then,
the fingers ... Nothing but a breath.

The ear is usually solid, I think.
The little body
is hollow.

We doubt, and are doubted. But it must be borne.

One begins with so little—collecting, sweeping.
Or seeing it, just seeing.

Months of dust. I'd have thought
we all would have been there.

Before his death, you know.
Or maybe nearby.

How will he find me?
Floating in blackness,

we took shelter. "I've seen him."
"Have you seen the end?"

Everybody wants a brother. They
swim in the blood. I want a grave. It was early

at first. Just the two dates. Blood is like that.
"Just a little further."

"Surely the people
is grass."

We were climbing but,
because we had the rakes,

we had to stop every little while and
do some raking.

Dear When-you-stop-you-will-feel,

Black, the color of space, mourning,
is green for rain. As if a legend to a map,
I saw the room and
wanted the life.

Wool men! we must consider:
what beauty means in the moth's world.
Come this far. Look briefly
into the past. Living in a house inside a house,

you receive a transmission of "meaning" energy
you cannot decipher.

Nothing marks the turn.

I was going to drive a train across the country.
And then a ship, across the sea.
She came to see me off. It was a little caboose
that I was driving. She asked me what was wrong.

I told her
that I'd had a dream. The ship was going to sink.
She said: "Remember—when you were a boy?
And we used to do the Magic of Believing?"

To begin a journey.
He set out (depart) to prove his point.
To set one's mind at rest.

There's a hole
in the middle of life (the body).
The flashbacks will remind us.

Set down. To write.
Or copy, to consider.
To humiliate or humble, set down in heavy fog.

To cause to pass into the given,
to set a prisoner free.

I was myself, to join what had been separate.
To translate without moving, "foliate."

Your blonde guitar, my plaster Buddha.
500 lbs. of perfect pitch.

So many passwords!
Emits
Veining

Inconclusive, in the shape
of the stain

He hears it! No—he sees

The heat makes waves
There is no water in this ground
And I promised to be brave

That's the sound: click. That's the sound we call "click." A girl who is nine plays a nine-year-old girl. A woman who is 50 plays a woman. With the skeleton inside. Gradually we realized.

First I was setting fire to the house, but we didn't want the authorities to know. So I was setting small fires. Setting the blue rug in the living room on fire in several spots. I asked my mother, should we try to save anything?

We can begin with the projection.

—What would illustrations of the inner life tell?
—It was forbidden, but there was no wall.

The river flowed out of the garden and divided
into four. Meaning: rapid or sudden, broad, bursting forth,
and fruitful. Possibly who floods in winter rains.

We were fighting
for the chimney field.
It's a landmark, you know how people are.

Separate the river from the blood.
Where the gate first split from the Latin, meaning "go away."
Because people have been burned for having views.

Dear within, I was seeing from a distance.
It stayed small for quite a while.

The giant takes us
down. A man with no arms.
Unbreakable.

What made today
is concordant,
transforms
the brief decisive phase we call fear.

I look to that whited-over part and see a face.
Then I look to the black and
see the same face.

There were tunnels…chambers
beneath some of the sidewalks…page after page of places…

The last thing you think of.
Won't be my fluffy blonde hair.

We have his ear.
He was the first boy I knew. The liberation.
Which I remember
from sand. The pail shape. The whole world's washed out.

These words: take refuge.
What I mean by dream in this case is
his last dream.
And you see no land, you're that far away.

Someone coughs
in my first life.
Someone must have noticed
how like you he is . . .

First you can't be heard
Then you can't hear
Then you can't dial
Then you can't turn it off

You pose a question, I repeat it.
And as always with speech, one is blind.

As a reflector, as of cloth or
thick flecked glass, as slats—
You asked though

about the self.
There were fireflies,
and the corn cut to the nubs. The windows
shook, we saw a flash of light . . .

then the tiniest
feckles
of rain

after we waited
all day.

That hard thread
between us.

Is it gold? Do I have to be
so outshined by my curtain?

Opened,
especially by breaking.

people who would die
people who would almost

die and
who would be injured

My dad was in the water.
Across an unprecedented space.

It would rain
for days, they said

he'd come home.
[*lists the father's wounds*]

That hard thread
is a bone. Is made of bone.

When I was
alone,
a girl,

the first loss,
between tunnels . . .

I didn't need so much.
I'd eventually get hungry.

I had a disease. Also I was drowned, also saved.

Put your hand
on my heart, a solid or

solid phase.
This is the foresight.

You might think of smoking, singing together...

These were our neighbors, who rescued the injured.
The women are all barefoot,
the men too.

And he's walking—
right into his shadow.
Arms extended, open as a field.

I have a lace veil on, and so does B, but we are not the bride.

"How are your eyes?" I say. She asks me
if I want to see. But I know they are just holes now.

They're taking the boats out of the water.
The sound of time passing the old notes.
Rereading our old mail, a place
to be remembered.

And if my brother
should call to me?

                              Of other riders,
                                  speak softly

                        Across the plains of America

                        Of other riders, their complex
                                      unhappiness,
                                            stuck
                           in readiness, anchored
                                     in cement

                        Dropping brightness, dropped
                                   to the sea bed

                        Of other riders, do not anchor

The world was ending, and everybody knew.
We lined up to say goodbye.

I saw some people out on the bridges.

One guy said don't worry—when it comes,
there'll be nothing left.

The big glass frame is worth something. Are they traveling together? are we traveling? We used to work until the chemicals were actually exhausted. What is faith but a picture that we carry, where the memories of everyone are stored. A stair is missing. Let us know our end. Let us know our end and the number of our days. This is how he talks to me, a tree losing its leaves.

The first light has a reason.

Someone asked, what is dying? And someone at my side said: "He's gone."
Almost at once, it's a story.

To fit,

as words
to music.
A spell, a round, a turn,
a quarrel.

What led.
Is it fog?

Something between us and the world.

Tired of "man's"
and the thousands of years

pound a cooling metal into shape.
The numbers
pile up,
like ideas.

"Be passerby."

To put or to apply,
to set fire to a house, or

what is this dust we're shoveling?

One, effort to restrain evil.
Two, effort to abandon evil.
Three, effort to develop good.
Four, effort to maintain good.

The other 20 hours are just dark
"the long brown path"
a piece of ground, landmined
by both sides

because I wanted what you had.

A turn,
a mordent,
a melodic
argument, a flag
Climbing
in the hard black
shoes
Dragging a stone
The transition
Alms
That's when I found out my insurance was worthless
Life had other qualities
Because people disappear from the earth
A green we did in seven values

Some days, I expect you. Sometimes it's a limited depth of field that you want. Truth, facts, the true story, the real picture. Why do we hate? Sure.

Dear friend, I can believe in the influence of Mars as fully as I can in the aorta. It's all invisible, in a normal day—though felt, as rhythm or excitement or pressure. You have the plate you can't drink from. And that one's missing an arm. And making art, too, is a kind of disappearing. A bucket with holes, on purpose.

Let's decide where we'll go if the house catches fire.
What we carry? Big shadow of a fly, years of pining.

At twilight, haunting the old homes.
Looking for the lamps once lit in rooms.

What you feel watching someone be lost for a while.
To bear a light for a person on a dark street.
To set one's dog on a stranger.

But
you see,
I am very old.

And there were eyes
in the wall.

I am not
a magnetic. Surely not. For my sight
dispersed.

If we haven't beauty
or wealth
or even goodness to save us…

Be brave but—
say there was a fire.

We should not shamelessly trample
upon one another.
I said "He's my brother"?

I don't know why I would have said that.

In calling, get ready.

Dear, there is a bridge between the middle and the end.
Designed by winds, caused to flex.

Fate includes both falling to another
level, as in falling from windows, stairs, or ladders,
and same level falls such as slipping,
or stumbling.

But remember when I asked if you were carrying an umbrella
and I asked you what you felt and I think there was a blind
person, sitting near you.
It's very strange
not to be writing,

not even to be drawn to it.
A lot of time
just at the piano,
an old upright that came with the house.
Just some old pieces I knew once, but I feel it quickens me.

Some keys don't strike fully and the surfaces are curling.
They don't use ivory anymore.

All art arises from longing. The love
we call the last four things.

She's been dead. She's come too far.
How tired she is!

Even the soldiers have to look away.

What I wanted, it wasn't for remembering. A broken liquid, like blood. The "next" with the description of how big it really is. Dear friend, don't be from the past.

Once we went under a tree, to get out of the rain—a thick tree, we waited there a while. That day, I don't think anybody cried.

Later, walking down the road. I still have the knife in my hand, but now it isn't made of gold. Punctuation's a resemblance question: latent, suppressed, subliminal, sleeping. Sometimes there's a word that can't be used. Dormant, inherent, instinctive, involuntary. Listen, keep in touch, I know you won't. The most vulnerable moment is the moment of the change. Four frames. Hold the strip to the light, "the higher plane." Released the shutter, what I wanted from a picture.

My wish is—I see now. That mesh.
Must be as strong as bullets.

For reducing the speed, distributing the light
of a lamp. Dear within, dear second.

You see a building cut in half, its rooms exposed.
How vulnerable a building is,
how simply cut away.

Born on this earth,
we're all alone tonight.
The sphere of mortal life, the fruiting spike, the ear.

Stand there.
I'll take your photograph.

56 DAYS

It's not that I can tell the future or know what's going to happen in the world. But I can know that certain things are never going to happen. Fortuity, take note.

Have you ever stood near a fire—a big fire? It's surprisingly loud. And hot. Of course, it's hot. I was thinking maybe I should buy a piece of tin to hide the baby, to protect the baby.

We come down from the mountains. We brought eggs. Proverbs. If you see in a field, or in any stretch of dirt, clover. Who buries a treasure. To him, it means "pause." To me, it means "others." Every contact leaves a trace.

She considers a field. The lie the camera tells about that moment is a better reminder than the memory of the moment could have been. The tie that holds you to your group—first you must accept: it's uncontrollable.

Writing toward you, through the pages between us. (Claps for the translation. That's the math.) The same things attract us. Birds, the train, listening, sleeping. Tension is shown with music. Sex with undressing and music. The use of wind. Daily routine is shown with music, and food. Bridges, doors.

I found a small dark rug on top of a junk pile on the curb and dragged it upstairs. Scrubbed it with a stiff brush and water. "Things are right in front of us," he says. "Why make them up?"

The pattern inside the eye. Long periods of gray. As if the prayers belonged to the person. Could be seen, later, in a display case: "her prayers." Makes her arms strong.

Tonight when the power went out, I put on my coat and walked into the lane. A woman spoke, I answered in her language. She had a lantern, I had a small flashlight. The sky was overcast and pale; the air, strangely mild. I looked around for a minute, then came back inside. There were candles and matches in a kitchen drawer. I lit a candle and sat down. I made a list of unavailable resources—various protections, youth. Every time a car drove by, I imagined the driver was fleeing our powerlessness. I wished I still smoked.

Men are trading their bullets for worms.
"I spent a lifetime building."

We come down from the mountains. We brought eggs, a table, a windowshade. There were times when we couldn't bring anything. So many people.

As you were walking up the hill and I was walking down, we almost passed each other. But I grasped your arm and backed up. You said: "This is what I look like now."

Did he spit on the floor? Sometimes I didn't wash for days. And things just lying there—where I left them. Like the moon. Like the trash on the moon.

Please come and take me out of here (Hasn't eaten)
Maps for everywhere.

Dear E, I'm glad we got a chance to talk. It was not as nice to see you as I thought

The bedlam of fatigue.

Sheep? in the middle of the city? This is the dream I have sometimes.

When they explain what they've learned about sleep, they never tell the part I need to know.

"One snowy night." When I hold the baby.

When I hold the baby I feel so good. I never felt so good.

She considers a field. She considers a field and buys it. Let her have the fruit of her hands.

We come down from the mountains. Yellow trees, green trees. I was leaving Earth but, before I did, I had to get rid of all my animals. My main one, my main model for behavior, was my snake. He was attached to the bottom of my foot but had become dangerous seeming and I was afraid he would bite me if he got the chance. My sister was there and I said, "Before I leave, I have to get rid of all my animals," thinking maybe she'd help me. I said, "My horse, my frog, my snake…" but didn't mention I was worried about how to dislodge my snake safely. As I was waking up, I thought of going to a place where they could give the snake a shot to knock it out or even kill it before they tried to get it off my foot. Which seemed like a pretty good idea, though inconvenient.

I understand if I said I've been crying for three days straight, that would always be the wrong thing to say. The word-system comes down. "She made a beautiful bride." Swore swear, hid hide, and so on. Slept sleep. Everything is in the distance.

Gloves, hands, the representation of hands—these are the spaces I have in mind. A miserable life among the sheep. In those heels? Are we talking about you then? Shouldn't you be wearing a ring? How did you get into this state?

She stays behind and gathers meaning. I will cover many examples of escaping. This is how I learned to make pictures.

To make it darker, press harder. The eye fills in what it knows. Ships, their sails, the wind puffing them out. And a tooth. The tooth with its shape. It has the same shape inside itself.

Her favorite things to draw were the tall ships and the tooth. "I'm so used to the nice legs the tooth has."

Consider the conditions of happiness. How much money would be enough? Most believe that men are compelled by two impulses. It's a convention, like closing the eyes of the dead to let them rest. Who buries a treasure. Photographs can survive water, for instance. If you were to submerge a box.

All those weird places we were going to live. When you got sad, I drove you around for a while instead of taking you home and brought you past each one of those houses.

Dan downstairs was quiet. I didn't hear his voice all day. I wondered—if something was wrong with Dan. Maybe he got sober, or was grieving.

Incident, occurrence, happening, chance: the medium of our progress. I see a field and it's full of grain. I look across it, beyond the reach of roads. I can see because it's flat. Trees? No, there's no edge. Yellow. It's a drawing. My sister kept it for me. No, I drew it from memory. I mean—when I drew it, I had never seen a field.

It begins in trouble, like all romance. There's a bad guy, a good guy, a handsome kid, some beautiful young women, there's a dog—the thing about dreams is, there's a plot. Full of sex, antibiotics. In the middle of a comeback, safe as ghosts.

Her horse lay down beside her. That's what my horse would do.

My father gave me my first camera. That's how I started taking pictures. I made a darkroom for myself at home, in the half-bath upstairs. They call it a half-bath now. I don't know what we called it then. It was like a closet with a toilet and a tiny sink. My parents let me paint the ceiling and the walls flat black. I had a job after school so I had a little money. I bought a cheap enlarger, trays, tongs (never used them), a safelight, a timer. I would open up a folding table in there after I closed the door—then it all fit.

I was enthralled with my black room, and the equipment and the chemicals. Even the names: the Fixer, the Stop Bath, the Orbit. Shaking the tray in the safe red dark, I was happy—watching the image come up—gray shapes collecting into streets or faces—

I'm not sure I can give you these sentences.

— I keep getting words like "invisible." Oh, I know what it is: "buried." So, when he stopped listening to God, was that when the trouble began or when it ended?

— The camera has two purposes: one is to help the person holding it to see. The other, simply to draw light into itself.

He reminds me of someone. I forget. Look at their eyes, these guys in spurs—do I say this every time? A million tiny names. And awards, attached with tiny pins. Those tiny gold pins. Voicings so wide apart, all you can do is pick a few. In which case, asks. Where he lives. Where we live. "I hate myself when I'm with you."

Puts it out on the floor, like Pollock. As children, we were asked to feel his pain. Our shadows tried themselves on every surface.

"Show love. Hold it up to heaven." This was called "the light of day." You can look at things with a camera. I call it "there is room for me."

— I like a big ship. You know, ships. They're great. They're giant.

— Large ships. Not like sailboats?

— Oh no, there's no sails. No. Powered by a motor or, I don't know… whatever they used to do, not sails. But they're not modern. They're big. You steer them with a giant wheel. That's all I know.

— You have the urge to steer one?

— Yeah, I do. With a giant wheel. I'd just be there. I'd be a little small, compared to the wheel, and I'd be steering it. It'd be great. There'd be a big map. A map with stars on it. We would navigate by the stars. The stars would be very bright—that's how we'd know where we were.

— Would you have a crew?

— They would be below.

— The ship is white. Mainly white, it has some blue.

— It's at sea?

— Of course. Just water everywhere. At night. With the stars.

— You'd be steering your ship.

— At night would be the main time.

— How about being on the shore when someone else is on the ship?

— I wouldn't. I wouldn't do that again.

— Did it ever happen?

— Oh, it always happens. To everyone. That's life.

New Year's Eve. Protecting that indefinitely prolonged bright edge. Twice I made you a honey cake. Once with coffee, once with tea.

No honey in the house tonight. No eggs. And you? Catch your death.

Tension is a form of dust.

Belief resembles knowledge (he says). I was explaining to someone that what *I* meant was: my eyes fell out like stones. To the ground, two brown stones. Safe as a shell on a shelf of shells. I leaned up against him a little. "You're not dead anymore."

He gave me a worn patterned rug to take with me. Whenever anything went wrong, he said, I could put my hands on that rug. I had the baby. I hadn't planned on going with a baby. But look at her, so quiet. She sleeps, nearly all the time.

The world wasn't coming to an end exactly. I was living in a supermarket. I had a few things from our life. I had the old reel-to-reel and I thought possibly, just with things I had, I could make a tape.

— "Faith" isn't always replaced by "faith in nothing."
— What does replace it then?
— It's not replaced.

Air (cool, warm, salty)
Water (ocean, river, lake)
Clouds (gray or white, silver lining, also at night)
Trees (green, yellow, red)
Rain (warm)
Sun (warm)
Farmland (brown, green, patterns)
Beach (walk, lie down)
Birds (all kinds)
Bridges (wood, metal, stone, suspension)
Islands (with trees, with a house)

First, you have a little sea inside you. A little sea and a little fish, in the sea. Just a tiny fish but then it grows, it starts to move around. It wants to get out. The sea can't stay inside you—it has to come out. And the little fish comes with it.

And then you have the little being. The little being in the world. Everybody loves their little baby. It's a lot of work, yes, but you're in a trance—you're in a trance of love. You get sick of it, sure—but you're still in the trance. Unless you hate the baby for some reason. But that didn't happen to me.

— Would you call these nightmares?
— No, they're just regular dreams. Afterwards, you forget.

Do a dangerous thing and you're in danger. That's how it works.

I was a child and he was my young uncle. It's too close, too deep. We could make a life. Fuck tripods, family, humans. We could make a life, a room. The red goes black very quickly. We all plugged in. We see his maleness now, thin as water. The embedded promise, widespread chords. A hundred shadows on the platform.

Trespass? A question to offer: Are signs adequate? Drinking water adequate? Restrooms operational, parking adequate?

How many rockets fell on the city today? We come down from the mountains. Yellow trees, green trees, swift river. Farmlands, warm rain. People travel with us. Machines that mine imaginary gold.

He gets to know the room. So he can navigate it when his sight is gone. A guard for what the bare hand should not touch. To be human? You have to keep doing it. You can never see what things are made of. And it's all so hard to believe in—you know…atoms? You're just here, out of nowhere. Then you go back into nowhere. And even every night you *beg* to go back. Just to make it stop for a while. Even though all you really want to do is stick around. That's what it's like.

"Even the stones in the field are dreaming about money." He's crossing. Near the cut point.

Fortuity, take note of the values around you. They're burying the suit.

At home, they've reorganized the kitchen. That means stories. We know the plot already. But even if we could go back, we couldn't live in that light. The previous light.

Amidst all the things we were chewing, there was one hard thing.

I'm no expert on fire. How it smells depends on what burns. People say it, but they don't know what it means: grease the wheels. This morning, as I fit the leader in the spool, I could feel it was the last time. The roll of Ilford was a little past its date. The familiar motion of advancing the film. I feel I should be able to recognize the future. I thought I'd make use of all the lenses today.

Using an old man's camera, I assumed it was a temporary thing for me. But his camera became my camera then, for years. And if it turns you into an observer...what *should* the life of an artist be like? Pining behind shields, sleeping with the lights on, the white dress rotting in safekeeping. She must be able to offer help to others. Puts her hands to the pane. I worked, I vow, I want an individual. This hapless window. And yet another minute of your time.

I've seen all a heart could desire. Yellow trees, swift river. Who we were. When they had a party next door, when a storm came. When we lay down together in the early afternoon. You can't ask this of me.

The answer is the wrong place at the wrong time. The wrong country, the wrong father, the wrong street, the wrong night.

Rest near the surface without sinking.
The trouble sleeps. She wakes into dark.

She can laugh at the days to come.
She is like the ships. Invisible.

I have a baby with me. Not mine, like a plant. "Nature boy."
His hair is green and black, fernish. Who's driving?

Everybody wants to look.
But they're protected, by nets.

Am I taking good enough care of him? Not mine.
And he's so tiny.

We come down from the mountains. Yellow trees, green trees, swift river. Farmlands, warm rain. Birds, all kinds. Proverbs. She considers a field. Who would bury a treasure would bury herself. But all that's a long time ago.

— And no one knew you?
— I was hard to know. I lied. I had to.
— They say you're always sad.
— There are a few things I'm afraid of. Quite a few, actually. I'd like to sleep. But if I have to do this the whole time I sleep . . .

Then suddenly resistance in the middle of a turn.

Someone was there to take a picture.

ABOUT THE AUTHOR

Ahsahta Press published KATE GREENSTREET's first book, *case sensitive,* in 2006. She is the author of several chapbooks as well, most recently *This is why I hurt you* (Lame House Press, 2008). For more about her, see kickingwind.com.

Ahsahta Press

SAWTOOTH POETRY PRIZE SERIES

NEW SERIES

Ahsahta Press

Modern and Contemporary Poetry of the American West

This book is set in Apollo MT type with Abadi MT Condensed Light titles
by Ahsahta Press at Boise State University
and manufactured according to the Green Press Initiative
by Thomson-Shore, Inc.
Cover design by M & K Greenstreet.
Book design by Janet Holmes.

AHSAHTA PRESS

2009

JANET HOLMES, DIRECTOR

A. MINETTA GOULD

KATE HOLLAND

BREONNA KRAFFT

MERIN TIGERT

JR WALSH

JAKE LUTZ, INTERN

ERIC MARTINEZ, INTERN

NAOMI TARLE, INTERN